Really Silly
JOKES

By **Cyl Lee**

BIG BUDDY

JOKES

Big Buddy Books
An imprint of Abdo Publishing
abdopublishing.com

abdopublishing.com

Published by Abdo Publishing, a division of ABDO, PO Box 398166, Minneapolis, Minnesota 55439.
Copyright © 2017 by Abdo Consulting Group, Inc. International copyrights reserved in all countries.
No part of this book may be reproduced in any form without written permission from the publisher.
Big Buddy Books™ is a trademark and logo of Abdo Publishing.

Printed in the United States of America, North Mankato, Minnesota.
082016
012017

THIS BOOK CONTAINS
RECYCLED MATERIALS

Illustrations: Sunny Grey/Spectrum Studio

Coordinating Series Editor: Tamara L. Britton
Contributing Editor: Katie Lajiness
Graphic Design: Taylor Higgins

Publisher's Cataloging-in-Publication Data

Names: Lee, Cyl, author.
Title: Really silly jokes / by Cyl Lee.
Description: Minneapolis, MN : Abdo Publishing, 2017. | Series: Big buddy jokes
Identifiers: LCCN 2016944865 | ISBN 9781680785142 (lib. bdg.) | ISBN
      9781680798746 (ebook)
Subjects: LCSH: Wit and humor--Juvenile humor.
Classification: DDC 818/.602--dc23
LC record available at http://lccn.loc.gov/2016944865

How did the telephone ask his girlfriend to marry him?

He gave her a ring!

A puddle!

4

Did you hear about the wooden car with the wooden wheels and the wooden engine?

It wooden go!

What did the window say to the door?

What are you squeaking about? I'm the one with the pane!

Why did the apple go out with a fig?

Because it couldn't find a date!

How did the chewing gum cross the road?

It was stuck to the chicken's foot!

Can February March?

No, but April May.

What do people do in clock factories?

They make faces all day!

What do you call a nervous celery stalk?

An edgy veggie!

What did the shy pebble say?

I wish I was a little boulder.

What letters are not in the alphabet?

The ones in the mail!

Woman: Excuse me, waiter, is there spaghetti on the menu?

Waiter: No, madam, I wiped it off.

What did the picture say to the wall?

I've got you covered!

Did you hear about the mad scientist who put dynamite in his fridge?

It blew his cool!

Why is Russia a very fast country?

Because the people are always Russian!

What happened when the wheel was invented?

It caused a revolution!

Why did the baker stop making doughnuts?

He got sick of the hole business!

What has four wheels and flies?

A garbage truck!

Why did the pig go to the casino?

To play the slop machine!

Why did the cookie go to the doctor?

He felt crumb-y.

How do you prevent a summer cold?

Catch it in the winter!

What do penguins use instead of napkins?

Flap-kins.

What did 0 say to 8?

Nice belt!

Where does satisfaction come from?

From a satis-factory.

If all your clothes were stolen,
what would you go home in?

The dark!

15

A best-smeller!

Why did the boy throw his clock out the window?

So time would fly.

Bobby: Where's your mom from?

Johnny: Alaska.

Bobby: Don't bother I'll ask her myself.

What did the light say when it was turned off?

I'm delighted!

Why did the cabbage win the race?

Because it was a head!

What is a baby's motto?

If at first you don't succeed, cry, cry again.

What do you take before every meal?

A seat!

Two cupcakes are baking in the oven. One cupcake says to the other, "Isn't this great! We're turning such a lovely golden brown." The other cupcake screams…

"Ahhhhhh! A TALKING CUPCAKE!"

Why did the scientist install a knocker on his door?

He wanted to win the no-bell prize!

What did Snow White say to the photographer?

Some day my prints will come!

How much does it cost a pirate to get his ears pierced?

A buccaneer!

Why were the suspenders sent to jail?

For holding up a pair of pants!

What did the old light bulb say to the new light bulb?

You're too young to go out tonight!

Why did the cook get arrested?

Because he beat an egg!

Why do ducks watch the news?

To get the feather forecast!

What happened when the lion ate the comedian?

He felt funny!

Why do dogs scratch themselves?

Because they know where it itches.

24

What did the digital watch say to the grandfather clock?

Look Pop, no hands!

How do locomotives hear?

Through their engineers!

If you drop a white hat into the Red Sea, what does it become?

Wet!

What do you call cheese that isn't yours?

Nacho cheese!

What did the hat say to the scarf?

You hang around while I go on ahead.

What did one eye say to the other?

Between you and me, something smells!

What do you call a bee with a quiet buzz?

A mumble bee!

What do you call a fairy who never takes a bath?

Stinkerbell!

What do you call a banana that has been cut in half?

A banana split.

Why did the little boy put candles on the toilet seat?

Because he wanted a birthday potty.

What vitamin helps you see?

Vitamin C.

Why did the man put his money in the freezer?

He wanted cold hard cash!

Why do bicycles fall over?

Because they are two-tired!

What is a robot's favorite snack?

Computer chips.

What does a dentist call his X-rays?

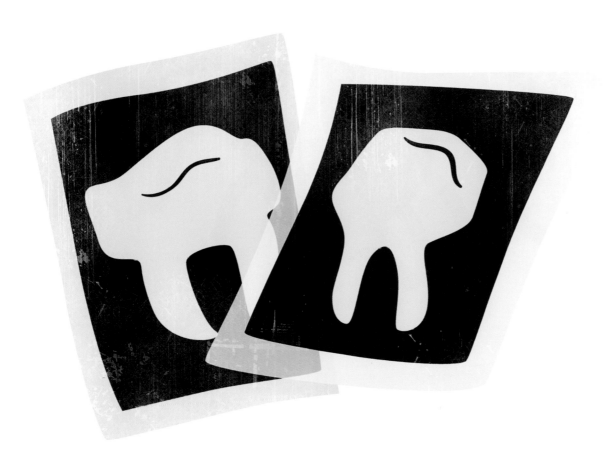

Tooth-pics!

31

WEBSITES

To learn more about Big Buddy Jokes, visit **booklinks.abdopublishing.com.** These links are routinely monitored and updated to provide the most current information available.